D0535920

DATE DUE

JUL 2 7 2004	AUG 0 5 2014	
SEP 1 9 2006	MAR 2 1 2017	
JUL 2 8 2010		
	AUG 1 2 2017	
AUG 1 4 2010	MAR 2 0 2018	
OCT 1 2 2010	APR 04 2019	
OCT 2 5 2011	APR 3 0 2019	
JUN 1 2 2012	AUG 1 3 2019	
AUG 2 0 2012	JUL 2 1 2021	
NOV 2 1 2012		
JUL 3 1 2013		
SEP 1 0 2013		
MAR 1 5 2014		
GAYLORD		PRINTED IN U.S.A.

JOSEPHINE COUNTY   3/04
LIBRARY SYSTEM
GRANTS PASS, OREGON

Swoop into the Nocturnal World of
OWLS

Josephine County Library
Grants Pass, Oregon

Published by Wildlife Education, Ltd.
12233 Thatcher Court, Poway, California 92064
contact us at: 1-800-477-5034
e-mail us at: animals@zoobooks.com
visit us at: www.zoobooks.com

Copyright © 2003 hardbound edition by Wildlife Education, Ltd.
All rights reserved. No part of this book may be reproduced in any form without written permission from the publisher.
Printed in China

ISBN 1-888153-93-8

Owls

Series Created by
John Bonnett Wexo

Written by
Timothy Levi Biel

Scientific Consultant
Arthur Crane Risser, Ph.D.
General Manager
Zoological Society of San Diego

Art Credits

Pages Eight and Nine: Trevor Boyer

Pages Twelve and Thirteen: Main Art, Trevor Boyer

Pages Twelve and Thirteen: Sidebar, Walter Stuart

Pages Sixteen and Seventeen: Main Art, Trevor Boyer

Page Sixteen: Bottom Left, Ed Zilberts

Page Seventeen: Top, Rebecca Bliss

Page Eighteen: Walter Stuart

Page Nineteen: Top, Walter Stuart; **Bottom,** Rebecca Bliss

Pages Twenty and Twenty-one: Main Art, Trevor Boyer

Page Twenty: Bottom, Raoul Espinoza

Pages Twenty and Twenty-one: Top, Rebecca Bliss

Page Twenty-one: Bottom, Walter Stuart

Photographic Credits

Front Cover: Stephen Dalton *(Photo Researchers)*

Pages Six and Seven: Hans Reinhard *(Bruce Coleman, Inc.)*

Page Eight: Doug Wilson *(West Stock)*

Page Nine: Top Left, William Boehm *(West Stock)*; **Top Right,**
Grant Heilman Photography; **Bottom Right,** Grant Heilman Photography

Page Ten: Top Right, Pekka Helo *(Bruce Coleman, Ltd.)*; **Middle Left,**
Liz and Tony Bomford *(Survival Anglia)*; **Middle Right,**
Frith *(Bruce Coleman, Inc.)*

Page Eleven: Top Left, Hans Reinhard *(Bruce Coleman, Inc.)*; **Top Middle,**
Hans Reinhard *(Bruce Coleman, Ltd.)*; **Top Right,** Ken M. Highfill
(Photo Researchers); **Bottom Right,** E. Breeze Jones *(Bruce Coleman, Ltd.)*

Pages Fourteen and Fifteen: Hans Reinhard *(Bruce Coleman, Inc.)*

Page Sixteen: Richard Leonhardt

Page Seventeen: Top, R.J.C. Blewitt *(Ardea London)*; **Middle Left,** C.F.E.
Smedley *(Natural Science Photos)*; **Middle Right,** Richard Leonhardt

Page Eighteen: Middle, George H. Harrison *(Grant Heilman)*;
Bottom Left, Michel Julien *(Valan Photos)*; **Bottom Middle,** Steven
Kaufman *(Peter Arnold, Inc.)*; **Bottom Right,** John Daniels *(Ardea London)*

Page Nineteen: Top, Em Ahart; **Bottom,** Jane Burton
(Bruce Coleman, Ltd.)

Page Twenty-one: Top Left, C. Allan Morgan; **Top Right,** Alan D. Briere
(Tom Stack & Associates); **Middle,** J. Senser *(Alpha/FPG)*;
Bottom, E. Breeze Jones *(Bruce Coleman, Ltd.)*

Pages Twenty-two and Twenty-three: Jack Bailey *(Ardea London)*

Back Cover: © Royalty Free *(Corbis)*

On the Cover: A European Eagle Owl

Contents

Owls are mysterious creatures. We often think of them as scary or even evil. They sometimes live in abandoned houses that may seem haunted. They fly without a sound through churchyards and cemeteries at night. In stories, they appear with witches, ghosts, and goblins. When we hear an owl's familiar "whooo...whooo...," it can send shivers down our spines. But why? Perhaps an owl's night habits make it seem spooky. Owls fly silently, without even a whisper of wings moving through the air. It's as though they appear out of nowhere—like ghosts on wings. Owls fly and hunt on the darkest of nights. Do these creatures of the night possess strange powers?

Owls possess *unusual* powers of sight and hearing, but they are not supernatural powers. They are natural adaptations that let them live most efficiently in their nocturnal environment. There is no reason to fear owls. Their habits make them helpful to humans. By hunting mice and other rodents, owls help to maintain a natural balance of plant and animal life. Without owls, rodents would overrun farmers' fields and storage barns.

More than 100 species of owls occupy a variety of habitats around the world. A few oceanic islands and the Antarctic have no owls. The world's owls come in large, medium, small, smaller, and smallest. For example, the Eurasian eagle owl—one of the largest—has a body that is two to three feet long, with a wingspan of up to five and one-half feet. The North American elf owl (the world's smallest owl) is five to six inches long and has a wingspan that measures slightly more than one foot.

Most male and female owls of the same species look alike, although females are usually larger. In some species, the female's colors help her to blend into the trees or grass where she makes her nest.

Baby owls, called chicks, stay with their parents until they are about three months old. They soon find their own hunting territories, where they may stay for the rest of their lives. Some owls can live 20 years or more.

Different kinds of owls live all around the world. They are found on every continent except Antarctica. Some owls live in cold climates, others live in warm climates. Owls make their homes in dry deserts, rain-soaked jungles, thick forests, and open plains. No matter where you live, you probably have several different kinds of owls living near you.

CHESTNUT-BACKED OWLET

SNOWY OWL

This owl lives in the cold, Arctic tundra at the top of the world. Its white feathers, barred with brown, blend in with the snow and mud of the frozen north. The long coat of feathers blankets the bird from its nose to its toes.

Tropical jungles are home to many small owls, like the one at left. With its small wingspan it can fly through the jungle without crashing into trees. Its reddish feathers are dark enough to let it hide in the shadows.

LONG-EARED OWL

Most owls live in heavily wooded areas. By day, they sleep in trees, where their colors make them hard to see. At night, many of them hunt for mice in the meadows and along the roadways near the forest's edge.

BARN OWL

A white face shaped like a heart makes this owl easy to recognize. Barn owls usually live near farms and hunt in open fields. Their long wings, spanning almost four feet, are suited to flight over open country where there are few trees.

Recognizing owls is easy. Just look for a round face, big eyes, and a sharp, hooked bill. The face is almost completely covered by two large discs, called facial discs. Many owls also have feathers sticking up on their heads that look like ears. These are called ear tufts.

It is not easy to tell one kind of owl from another. You have to look carefully. Look closely at the owls pictured here. See what differences you can discover in these owls before you read about them.

Do the facial discs of some owls look different than others? Do you see some owls with ear tufts and others without? Do the ear tufts all look the same? What other differences do you see? After you have studied these owls, read the captions and see how well you did.

GREAT GRAY OWL

Did you notice how big this owl's face is? It has the largest facial discs of any owl. Its unusually small eyes make the discs look even bigger.

PEL'S FISHING OWL

Did you notice anything different about the lower legs on this owl? They aren't feathered. Fishing owls don't need feathers on their legs to protect them from their prey. And it's easier to fish without wet feathers getting in the way.

Recognizing birds in the wild is tricky, because you don't always get a good look at them. If you saw this owl flying overhead, would you notice its gray color or the stripes under its wings? Would you see the ear tufts or the small, oval discs on its face? If so, you would probably know that this owl is an eastern screech owl.

EASTERN SCREECH OWL

MALAYSIAN EAGLE OWL

This eagle owl is easy to recognize. It has extremely long ear tufts that stick straight out on the sides of its head.

Ear tufts and facial discs form a "V" on the foreheads of these scops owls. Most scops owls have noticeable ear tufts and bushy feathers that cover their beaks like moustaches.

COLLARED SCOPS OWLS

This and the milky eagle owl are the largest of owls. The Eurasian eagle owl and the great horned owl of North America share similarities of habitat, vocalization, breeding biology, and appearance. Both have large ear tufts, and like most owls, their legs and feet are thickly covered with feathers that protect them from biting prey.

Compare this owl's face with the others shown here. Do the other faces look rounder? They should. Only bay owls and barn owls have triangular or heart-shaped faces.

BARN OWL

TAWNY OWLS, YOUNG AND ADULT

Young owls do not look like their parents. Adult tawny owls have reddish brown feathers, large heads, wide and round facial discs, and big, black eyes. Young tawny owls have fluffy white feathers and dark blue eyes. Which is the young owl in this picture?

*A*n owl's body is ideal for night living. Its superb senses help it to hunt in the dark. Owls have the best night vision of any creature on earth. Their hearing is even more remarkable. An owl can hear the tiny sound of a mouse stepping on a twig from 75 feet away!

Owls look the way they do because of these sharpened senses. Their heads have to be large because they have huge eyes and ears. The skull is broad so that both eyes look forward, which makes the owl's vision more accurate. Even the facial discs help the owls hear better!

Owls hear better than other birds. Most birds have small ear openings in their skulls. Many owls have very large openings surrounded by feathers that the owl can spread to funnel sound into the ear.

Their eye position gives owls good depth perception. Most birds have eyes on the sides of their heads. They have a wide visual field, but only see a tiny area with both eyes. An owl's eyes look straight ahead to have a broader range where vision overlaps. The orange areas show the *binocular*, or three-dimensional visual field of most birds *1* and of owls *2*.

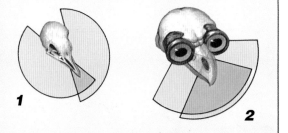

Most animals that are active at night have big eyes to catch almost all the light available. An owl's eyes are so big that they cannot be moved. The eyes are fixed straight ahead.

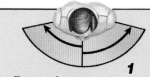

1

Because its eyes cannot move, an owl must keep turning its head to follow a moving object. An owl's neck is so flexible, it seems to be made of rubber.

Imagine that your eyes cannot move. You only see what is in front of you. To see to right or left, you must turn your head, but still you can see only what is ahead of you **1**.

2

An owl can turn its head so far to the right **2** that it sees what is behind it. It can keep turning until it is actually looking over its left shoulder! It can turn its head so far to the left **3** that it looks over its right shoulder.

3

An owl can turn its neck so far so fast, it sometimes looks as though the head is spinning like a top!

Starting with its head already turned as far as it will go one way, an owl can then turn its head a full circle and a half in the other direction **4**.

4

Ear tufts aren't ears at all. An owl's ears are holes hidden behind their facial discs and protected by movable skin flaps. An owl can move its facial discs back and forth to pick up sounds from different angles. With the aid of the flaps, the facial discs, and the soft feathers surrounding the ear, the owl can focus sounds from different directions and channel them into the ear. Owls whose two ears are irregular in shape and size can fine tune the focus to the *exact* direction and distance of a sound.

The wings of most birds have stiff feathers that make noise when they fly **1**. An owl's wing feathers have soft edges **2**, so that it flies more quietly. This lets the owl listen carefully for its prey, while flying close to it without being heard.

1

2

13

Hunting at night is something that owls do better than any other bird. When hawks and eagles sleep, owls take over. They hunt the same areas and many of the same kinds of prey. Because of the darkness, owls must use different hunting skills than the daytime hunters.

When they hunt, owls do not soar like eagles. They do not use long-range vision like hawks. Instead, they fly close to the ground, listening and watching for their prey in the dark.

To hunt, an owl perches silently on a branch. Then it watches and listens for movement below.

An owl's *talons*, or claws, are dangerous weapons. The way they stab and hold their prey works like the ice hook below, which stabs and holds slippery blocks of ice. Once an animal is in the owl's grasp, it rarely escapes.

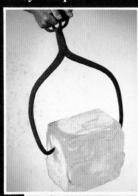

When an owl attacks, it spreads all eight of its toes as far as they will stretch. This gives the owl a better chance of grabbing its prey in the dark.

See for yourself why an owl spreads its talons so wide. Place a tiny wad of paper in front of you. Close your eyes and try to touch the paper using only one finger. Now try spreading all your fingers as wide as you can. You have a much better chance of striking the paper this way. That's the way it works for the owl, too.

When it sees or hears an animal below, the owl swoops down and flies close to the ground. As it gets closer and closer, it stops beating its wings and glides in for the attack.

After capturing its prey, the owl flies back to its perch. Unless it has something big, like a rabbit, it carries the prey in its bill.

Owls usually swallow their prey whole—even teeth, bones, and fur. If the prey is too large, the owl breaks it into pieces. But it still swallows bones and all.

The owl cannot digest everything that it swallows. Some things, like teeth, bones, and hair, are packed into *pellets* and spit out. If you find owl pellets and gently take them apart, you can see what an owl has eaten.

The sharp beak is used to tear pieces of meat that are too large to swallow whole. Although it looks dangerous, the bill is never used as a weapon. Owls always use their claws for that.

PELLET

PELVIS AND LEG BONES OF RAT

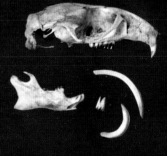

SKULL AND TEETH OF RAT

Owls can capture a wide variety of prey—not just rabbits and rodents. Many also catch birds. Fishing owls eat mostly fish. And eagle owls sometimes take young deer.

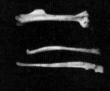

To order owl pellets:
Acorn Naturalists
17821 East 17th Street
Tustin, California 92781-2423
1-800-422-8886
www.acornnaturalists.com

Owls play **an important role** in nature. Whether we realize it or not, owls affect our lives every day. They help us by controlling rodents and insects. We tend to forget this, though.

We sometimes treat owls as our enemies. But they are really the enemies of insects, rodents, and small birds. If it weren't for owls and other predators, the numbers of these animals would zoom out of control. As it is, owls and their prey are locked in a constant fight for survival. Of course, owls must also compete with each other.

People often chop down old, rotting trees, where many owls like to nest. Some people help these owls by building nest boxes where owls can live. To learn how to build a nest box, ask for "Barn Owl Nest Box Plans" from:
Natural Resources Conservation Service
332 S. Juniper Street, #110
Escondido, CA 92025 (760) 745-2061

Every owl has its own territory, or hunting area. It usually patrols its "borders" to keep other owls out. However, owls of different species sometimes share the same territory. They get along by hunting at different times of day, or for different kinds of prey. A great gray owl, a Ural owl, and a tawny owl may share the same territory. The great gray owl is a daytime hunter. Despite its large size, it hunts almost entirely for little rodents called voles.

GREAT GRAY OWL

URAL OWL

The Ural owl can hunt by day or night. Instead of hunting for voles, it usually looks for larger prey, like squirrels.

A tawny owl that patrols the same territory also hunts voles, but avoids the great gray owl by hunting only at night.

TAWNY OWL

Owls help farmers by keeping rodents and small birds away. But farmers sometimes poison owls accidentally. When they spray their fields to kill weeds, insects, and rodents, they also harm owls. Owls eat the insects, rodents, and birds that have been poisoned. The more the owls eat, the more poison they consume.

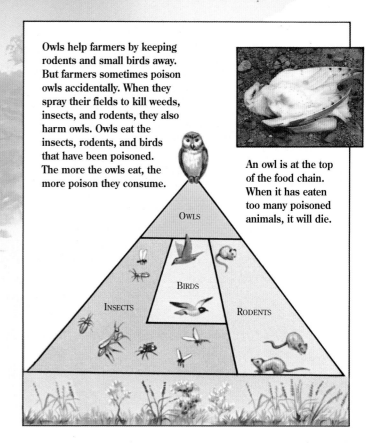

An owl is at the top of the food chain. When it has eaten too many poisoned animals, it will die.

OWLS

BIRDS

INSECTS

RODENTS

Owls don't like intruders. If they see one, they usually spread their wings, fluff up their feathers, and hiss loudly. This *threat display* is meant to scare intruders away.

Owls are the deadly enemies of small birds. Sometimes mobs of these little birds will all fly toward an owl at once. Usually the owl is startled, but not hurt. The small birds are just delivering a message: "We know you're there, so don't try sneaking up on us!"

A mother owl gives her little chicks constant care for almost three months. She feeds them, protects them from danger, and teaches them to fly and hunt. By the time the chicks are three months old, they must be expert hunters so they can leave their parents and find territories of their own.

The father owl often helps the mother raise their young. The father may even take his turn sitting on the eggs. After the eggs hatch, he goes hunting and brings back food for the whole family.

Considering how independent adult owls are, it is amazing to see how well mother and father owls cooperate.

When he thinks a female is watching him, he lands and drops his prey. With wings and tail outspread, he struts around the lemming.

In the spring, male owls behave in special ways to attract females. The male snowy owl carries a lemming in its beak and beats his wings wildly as he flies around.

It takes most young owls about six months before they look like adults. Spectacled owls (below) keep their beautiful white body feathers and dark faces for about *five years*.

The younger brothers and sisters in this family of spectacled owls are too young to fly. Can you tell which of them is the youngest?

The number of eggs an owl lays depends on its supply of food. In years when prey is scarce, the owl may lay no eggs at all **1**. If the number of prey is small, it may lay two or three eggs **2**. In years with plenty of food, there will also be plenty of eggs **3**.

1

2

3

If a female approaches him, he turns his back to her and hides the lemming with his wing. He continues to do this while she gradually moves closer. This may go on for hours, but slowly, they begin to accept each other.

YOUNG SCREECH OWLS

BARN OWL CHICKS

Owls nest in unusual places. Some small owls rely on woodpecker holes in trees and in giant cactus. Barn owls may choose barns, caves, or mines. Burrowing owls nest underground in the former burrows of prairie dogs, foxes, and ground squirrels. To ward off danger, the distress call of a burrowing owl chick sounds like the rattle of a prairie rattlesnake.

BURROWING OWL

This mother owl is teaching her month-old chicks to fly. With each flight, she increases the distance slightly. Flapping their wings wildly, the chicks try to follow her.

Owls have no fear when it comes to protecting their young. They swoop to attack anything that disturbs their nest and strike with their sharp talons.

Chicks usually hatch two days apart. The oldest chick grows up to be the strongest, because it gets most of the food. When food is scarce, only the oldest chick gets enough to survive. This assures that at least one of the young owls will live.

21

The future of most owls seems promising. People can help owls to survive. The first step is to learn about animals and nature. The second step is to teach others about the value of wildlife.

Owls and other predators will help us control pests, but we need to preserve their habitat so they have trees to live in and land where they can hunt. It's not always easy for people to leave wild places for animals when it conflicts with other human interests.

Throughout the 20th century, many of the world's forests were cleared to make room for cities and farms. Owls that prefer open spaces, like barn owls, just moved into barn lofts and the attics of old houses. Even many woodland owls, such as the tawny owl, the screech owl, and the long-eared owl, have adjusted to changes in their habitat. Other owls have not been so lucky.

The spotted owl lives in dense evergreen forests in the western United States. Because of its nocturnal habits and its diminishing numbers, this owl is seldom seen. By day, it roosts in the tall trees that people want to cut down for lumber. By night, it hunts mice, wood rats, moths, beetles, and even bats.

In the Pacific Northwest, entire forests have been cleared for their lumber. This practice has threatened the survival of the spotted owl. This owl's own gentle nature also puts it in danger. It does not attack intruders to its nest and makes no threats in defense of itself or its young. It is tame enough to be easily coaxed toward those who would further harm this endangered species.

The world's largest owls, the Eurasian eagle owls, are also in danger. These owls need large hunting territories and large prey, such as rabbits, ducks, and snakes. But the owls live in heavily populated areas of the world, where their prey is not easy to find.

We can help owls by setting aside wilderness areas where they can live. Forests can be selectively cut to leave corridors of trees for wildlife. (When a forest is clear-cut, it can cause erosion and flooding.) We can also enforce laws that protect owls from being hunted and senselessly killed. And if we must cut down trees, we can put up nest boxes (see page 12) that make it easier for some owls to live and reproduce near cities and towns. A wise old owl would say that by working together, we can build a promising future for owls the world over.

Index